Making Monsters Happy

Susan Gates

Illustrated by Steve May

Contents

Manu and the Werewolf

Manu had the coolest job in the world – he was a Monster Helper! Whenever monsters were unhappy, they would ask Manu for help. But making monsters happy isn't always easy ...

One day, Manu was walking through the park. Suddenly, a werewolf jumped out from behind a tree.

'Are you Manu?' he said. 'I need your help!'

'What's your problem?' said Manu.

'I'm human really, but I'm stuck in this scary wolf body. Now everyone runs away from me!'

'I don't know how to change you back to a human,' said Manu. 'But perhaps I can make you look less scary?'

Manu gave Werewolf his coat, scarf and bobble hat. 'Put these on,' he said.

Just then, two police officers walked by.
Werewolf smiled with his big wolf teeth.

'Hello,' he said.

'Help!' screamed the police officers,
running away. 'It's a monster!'

'It's no good,' sighed Werewolf. 'I still
look scary. It's so lonely being a werewolf.
I've got no friends and no home!'

Suddenly, Manu had another brilliant idea. 'Why don't you pretend you're a dog? Pet dogs have a great time!'

Werewolf cheered up at once. 'I could eat doggy treats! I could chase sticks!'

Werewolf tried his best to be a dog. He woofed. He sniffed at trees. He tried to play with the other dogs. But they all ran away!

Werewolf fetched a stick and carried it to a lady. She was so shocked that she fainted!

'Oh no!' howled Werewolf. He licked her face to try to wake her up. Just then, lots more police officers appeared.

'You monster!' they shouted. 'Stop eating that lady!'

'See?' Werewolf told Manu. 'No one likes werewolves. I'll *never* be happy!' And Werewolf ran away howling.

'Oh dear,' thought Manu. 'This is all going wrong!'

He ran after Werewolf and found him in a field nearby. A farmer was trying to round up his sheep, but they were running all over the place.

Werewolf ran to help the farmer. When they saw a big wolf, those sheep were as good as gold! Werewolf rounded them up in no time.

'Thank you!' said the farmer. 'You're a strange-looking sheepdog, but I don't mind. You're brilliant at rounding up sheep!'

The farmer patted Werewolf on his
big, hairy head. 'Will you come and live at
my farm?' he said.

'Woof! Woof!' said Werewolf, nodding
his head.

Werewolf jumped into the farmer's truck.

'Hooray!' thought Manu. 'Werewolf is
happy now!'

Werewolf stuck his head out of the truck window. He had a big smile on his face. He gave a big werewolf howl of happiness: 'Owwww-owww-owwww!'

Then he turned it into a doggy woof, just in time!

WOOF!

Manu and the Monster Tomato

Manu's grandad was on holiday and Manu was looking after his garden. Manu went into Grandad's greenhouse – and saw an amazing sight! A monster tomato plant filled the greenhouse.

'I need a drink of water,' it said.

'OK,' said Manu.

'Aren't you surprised I can talk?' said Monster Tomato.

'No,' said Manu. 'I've met all kinds of monsters.'

'I'm the cleverest tomato plant in the world!' boasted Monster Tomato. 'I know all my times tables *and* I can spell *Tyrannosaurus rex*.'

Manu gave it a drink of water.

'I'm really unhappy,' Monster Tomato told Manu. 'And when I'm unhappy, I eat people. I just can't help it.'

'That doesn't sound good,' said Manu.

'Don't worry, I won't eat *you*,' said Monster Tomato. 'You gave me a drink. You're my friend.'

Monster Tomato gave Manu a big hug.

I must help Monster Tomato be happy,
Manu decided. *It can't go around eating
people. What if it gobbles Grandad when he
comes back from holiday?*

'What will make you happy?' Manu
asked Monster Tomato.

'I want to be famous!' said Monster Tomato, waving its arms about. 'I am the cleverest tomato plant in the world! I should be a big star!'

Manu had no idea how to make Monster Tomato famous. But, just then, his mobile rang.

'Hi, Grandad!' said Manu.

'There's a Garden Show on Saturday,' Grandad told Manu. 'Can you take my tomato plants? I want them to win that big gold cup!'

'Would you like to win a big gold cup?' Manu asked Monster Tomato.

'Wow!' said Monster Tomato. 'That would make me *really* happy.'

'And then you won't eat people any more?' asked Manu.

'No way!' said Monster Tomato. 'I promise! I'll never eat people again!'

On Saturday, Manu and his dad loaded Monster Tomato on to a lorry. They drove through the town. All the people stared. Monster Tomato had a fantastic time. It waved at everyone, just like The Queen.

At the show, two judges went into the tent. Everyone else had to wait outside.

Manu was really worried. What if Monster Tomato didn't win? Would it eat the judges?

Suddenly, the judges came rushing out of the tent. They looked terrified.

Manu went into the tent. Monster Tomato had won everything – Best Tomato Plant, Best Monster Plant, Best Talking Plant ... It had even won the big gold cup for the Best Plant in the show!

Monster Tomato looked really happy.

'I'm a big star!' it told Manu. 'I'm
famous! I'm going to be on telly tonight!'

'What did you say to those judges?'
Manu asked Monster Tomato.

'I said,' Monster Tomato told Manu, 'if
you don't give me *all* the prizes, I'll eat you
for my dinner!'

Manu and the Mummy

Today was Manu's day off from helping monsters and he was enjoying a trip to the museum.

Suddenly, a mummy jumped out of a dark corner.

'Boo!' yelled the mummy, making a scary face.

'Hi,' said Manu, shaking the mummy's hand. 'How are you doing? My name is Manu.'

'My name is Mummy,' said the mummy crossly. 'Why aren't you screaming? Why aren't you running away?'

'Because I'm not scared,' said Manu.

Suddenly, Mummy started to cry. 'But I want to be scary!' he sobbed. 'I'm the most useless monster *ever*!'

'No, you're not,' said Manu, giving
Mummy a tissue. 'It's just that I'm used to
monsters. I meet them all the time.'

But Mummy wasn't listening. 'I couldn't
scare a kitten!' he sobbed. He stomped out
of the room.

'Watch out!' yelled Manu. Mummy's bandage had got trapped in a revolving door! Mummy was spinning around.

'Help me, Manu!' he screamed.

Manu rushed to help. But he was too late. All Mummy's bandages had come off!

Mummy was crying again. 'I'm even less scary now!' he sobbed.

Manu said, 'Quick! Let's go into this bathroom. We might find something to cover you.'

But all they found was toilet paper.
'This will have to do,' said Manu.
So he wrapped Mummy up from head to toe in pink, fluffy toilet paper.

'Do I look scary again?' Mummy asked Manu.

'Hmmm,' said Manu. 'I'm not sure if *scary* is the right word.'

Manu followed Mummy back to his glass case. Mummy climbed in.

A little girl came in with her dad. 'I don't want to look at any mummies,' she said. 'Mummies are really scary!'

Then she saw Mummy and ran over for a better look. 'This one isn't scary!' she told her dad. 'I like this pink mummy! He's really *cute*!'

Cute? thought Mummy, amazed. *No one has ever called me CUTE before*!

Soon, more children came running over to see the pink mummy. They crowded round.

'He's so fluffy!' one said.

'I like the pretty pink bow on his head,' said another.

They all said, 'He's the cutest thing in the whole museum!'

At last, the children went away. Manu thought, *Oh dear. Mummy will be really cross now. I didn't help a bit.*

But Mummy was ... smiling!

'Did you see how those children loved me?' he asked Manu. 'They called me cute!'

Manu said, 'But I thought you liked being scary?'

'Not any more,' said Mummy. 'Cute is the new me! Thanks, Manu! You've made me really happy!'

About the author

I was born in Grimsby. My mum was a tailoress and my dad is a guitar player. I've written over a hundred books for children. I like playing the guitar and going to the seaside. I now live in County Durham and have three adorable children. (I have to say that – they might read this book!)

In most monster stories, people run *away* from monsters. So I thought it would make a nice change when, in my story, Manu runs *towards* them. He does it because he wants to help. After all, monsters sometimes need help with their problems, just like the rest of us.